Casas De Banho • Bathrooms • 浴室 • Los Baños
ns • 浴室 • Banyolar • 화장실들 •
Badezimmer • Badkamers •
Casas De Banho • Bathrooms • 浴室 • Los Ba
s salles de bains • 浴室 • Banyolar • 화장실들
os Baños • Badezimmer • Badkamers •
I Bagni • שירותים • Casas De Banho • Bathroo
หลายห้อง • Les salles de bains • 浴室 • Banyo
Bathrooms • 浴室 • Los Baños • Badezimmer
anyolar • 화장실들 • I Bagni • שירותים • Casas
dkamers • ห้องน้ำหลายห้อง • Les salles de ba
De Banho • Bathrooms • 浴室 • Los Baños •
• 浴室 • Banyolar • 화장실들 • I Bagni • ם
Badkamers • ห้องน้ำหลายห้อง • Les salles de
asas De Banho • Bathrooms • 浴室 • Los

Colors for Living

BATHS

BY JENNIE L. PUGH WITH SANDRA RAGAN

DEDICATION

This book is dedicated to the colorful people in my life—
especially Ken and Allen.

First published in the United States of America by:
Rockport Publishers, Inc.
146 Granite Street
Rockport, Massachusetts 01966
Telephone: (508) 546-9590
Fax: (508) 546-7141

First Thailand edition 1995,
published by Rockport Publishers, Inc. for:
Page One (Thailand) Ltd
230 Soi Thonglor 8
Sukhumvit 55
Bangkok 10110
Thailand
Telephone/Fax: (662) 391-3657

First Singapore edition 1995,
published by Rockport Publishers, Inc. for:
Page One
The Bookshop Pte Ltd
Blk 4, Pasir Panjang Road
#08-33 Alexandra Distripark
Singapore 0512
Telephone: (65) 2730128
Fax: (65) 2730042

ISBN 1-56496-103-6

10 9 8 7 6 5 4 3 2

Art Director: Laura Herrmann
Designer: Nick Clark
Layout and production: KBB Design
Cover Photograph: Lanny Provo

Printed in Hong Kong

BATHS

Rockport Publishers, Inc.
Rockport, Massachusetts

TABLE OF CONTENTS

Photo: Paul Warchol

PREFACE

My favorite story illustrating the adage that good design begins with a well-thought-out concept happened one cold winter in the desert near Santa Fe, New Mexico. I was there visiting a friend who lived in a beautiful old adobe dugout. The first morning, I woke to the sound of Barbara stoking a wood-burning Ben Franklin—and saw a toilet seat leaning against one side of the stove. "Why is that there?" I asked. "Take this with you to the outhouse and you'll find the answer," she replied. Wrapped in my blanket, with the stove-warmed toilet seat in hand, I climbed a footpath to the cliff edge overlooking the Rio Grande River one hundred feet below. There, at the head of the path, was a small wooden building. As I entered, I discovered that one wall of this outhouse was glass: the wall overlooking the canyon! The desert presented me with its early morning palette; the adobes below glowed rose and the river winked with the hint of pale yellow to come. I will never forget that morning watching the sunrise over the Rio Grande, warmed and comfy. What could have been an uncomfortable inconvenience became a fun adventure because of color and design.

Vacations seem to be the time I notice baths the most, probably because I have more time to pamper myself. Washing off the road dust is one of the luxuries, and cere-monies, of travel. One bath that made me feel truly pampered was in a villa by the sea. The room had white-glazed, terra-cotta tiles whose irregular edges created an atmosphere that was at once primitive and luxurious. The colors and textures of a deep azure sunken tub—surrounded by a garden of giant philodendrons and orchids—created the same feeling as the glorious scenery I had traveled so far to see. As I stepped down into the water, jets began to ease the tension of the day's journey.

I marvel at bathrooms on sailboats, they intrigue my designer side. The space is always so small, and the fixtures are all interdesigned in clever ways. And no matter how tiny these seafaring baths are, they're pristine white and fitted out with brass and a teak floor grate, in keeping with nautical tradition. You, too, can incorporate a theme or historic period into your bath design.

Ask ten different people to describe the ideal bath and you'll get ten different answers. Baths can be locker rooms, dressing rooms, healing rooms, or even rooms of seduction. Baths are part of our daily ritual: we wake ourselves up there and prepare ourselves for sleep there. We brush our teeth, shave, put on make-up, apply Band-Aids to skinned knees, and keep our medications there. It is important that your bath's design and color be both a joy and an asset to you and your family.

Photo: Hickey-Robertson

INTRODUCTION

ESTABLISH YOUR DESIGN CRITERIA

A design is a goal or plan. I always begin my design plan with words. If you write a sentence or paragraph that describes your ideal bath then you will have a map to follow that will keep you on track in creating your design.

Some topics to consider are listed below. In addition to your goal, list your lifestyle needs, the style and colors of the rest of the house, and the elements you cannot change. The final ingredient will be your own style. Put that into words too, then use all of this information to write your design concept.

Remember, whether by design or default, the colors that appear in your bath will make a statement.

STYLE AND LIFESTYLE

Let's begin at the beginning. How many people use this bath? If crowds trek through, then it should be designed as a crowd pleaser: essentials placed within easy reach, and colors that don't show dirt. If only one person uses this bath, then it can make a stronger, more personal statement.

Does the room double as a guest bath? If so, perhaps you should consider a conservative palette. Do you want a room that will pick you up, or one that will calm you down? Warm colors will energize you; cool colors will bring serenity at the end of the day.

Sometimes there is a gap between imagination and practicality; your image of the ideal bath may not work for everyday use. If you collect all of the criteria first and then design to that, you will end up with a bathroom that is both functional and beautiful.

THE REST OF THE HOUSE

This room does not exist in a void; baths come with a whole house attached to them. Do you have a furniture style or historic period decor that should be reasonably represented here? Bath colors can continue the statement begun in other rooms. Consider the colors of the adjoining rooms and the visual flow— or shock—of walking from one space to another.

COLOR CHALLENGES

In bath design you may be challenged by a pink tub or blue tile that is already there. If there is a color that has to stay, make it the first color of your palette. Is your bath very small or oddly shaped? Light, bright colors will give it an open, airy feeling. By using different colors on different surfaces you can make some areas come forward and others recede.

How much light comes into the room? If you have the luxury of lots of natural light you can use more saturated colors. If the light source is primarily electric, check color swatches indoors rather than out. Changes in light can dramatically change a color.

YOUR OWN STYLE

Baths are private places where design can be particularly expressive. Why not use your favorite country, favorite vacation spot, or your dream castle as inspiration?

Sit quietly for a few minutes and think. Imagine the place or event you like most. What colors come to mind? What textures? Is the room brightly lit or dim? Are the surroundings luxurious or Spartan? Use these colors and textures to make the room your own.

MAKE COLOR WORK FOR YOU

Once the design criteria is determined, the next step is knowing how to use color to create the picture you want.

HOW WE RECEIVE COLOR

Colors affect us physically and emotionally; some even affect our involuntary reflexes. Red has been shown to raise blood pressure while its tint, pink, actually has a calming effect. We also respond to color emotionally, based on our experiences. Many responses to color seem to be generally universal. Perhaps we lovingly remember the color of a favorite automobile, or a not-so-favorite school uniform. Cultures also dictate associations with colors. Your own color associations will be useful to you as you study the color descriptions.

COLOR AND PERCEPTION

Perception is how the eye reads color. If you place a two-inch square of white beside a two-inch square of dark green, the white square will appear larger. In interior design, these perceptions of weight or size or distance can be used to manipulate the illusion of space.

From the classical painters we learned that grayed colors create the illusion of distance. If the bath you are designing is shallow, painting the wall opposite the door a grayed color will make it appear to recede. Color breaks at the ceiling or wainscoting are the perfect places to perform this magic. In bathrooms that are chopped up by windows and doors, use a brightly colored tile line around the room to move the eye through the space.

COLOR WHEEL

The color wheel is the most useful tool to help you understand the relationships of color—one to another, and of groups of colors together. Use the wheel as you explore possible color combinations for the bath.

Hue is the formal term for color, or color name, such as red, yellow, or blue. *Value* is the relative lightness or darkness of a color. Colors with white added are *tints* and colors with black added are known as *shades*. *Saturation* is the intensity or brightness of a color, and *temperature* is the perceived warmth or coolness of a color.

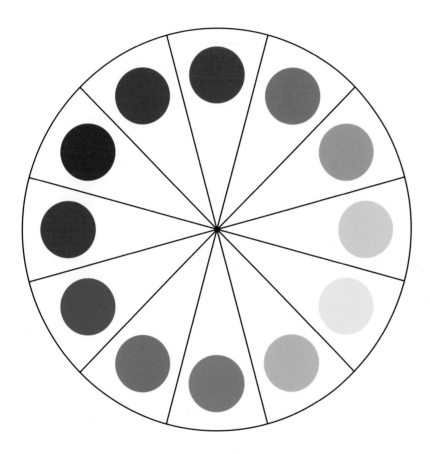

● BASIC COLOR SCHEMES

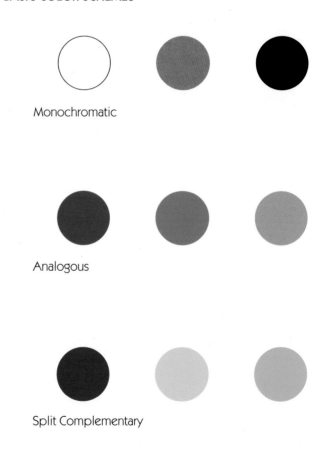

Monochromatic

Analogous

Split Complementary

COLOR THEORY

Color theory explains how colors relate to one another. The color wheel above presents colors in their logical sequence. Once you have decided on a base color, understanding color theory gives you a vocabulary of color to work with.

Triad

Photo: Dennis Jenkins

Colors are combined to form various schemes. A *monochromatic* color scheme uses variations of one color, or only white, black, and gray in combination. *Analogous* color schemes use three colors, or their tints and shades, which are next to each other on the color wheel. An analogous scheme might contain red, red-orange, and yellow, or red-orange, yellow, and pink (which is a tint of red).

A *complementary* color scheme employs colors from opposite sides of the color wheel, for example, purple and yellow. A *split complement* scheme using the same example would pair the two colors next to yellow on the color wheel—yellow-orange or yellow-green—with purple. A *triad* color scheme uses three colors, or their shades or tints, that are equidistant on the color wheel, such as red, yellow, and blue.

Photo: R. Greg Hursley

ENTER COLOR

Picture a storm rolling across the sea. What are your responses to the dark grays and blues? Remember a walk through the woods on a beautiful day. Do the scents, sounds, and colors conjure up special memories? Our senses call on former experiences. Color is constantly present in interpreting the world around us.

Through the ages colors have been integral to science, art, religion and myth, and celebration. In our society we have developed both positive and negative responses to any given color. Use these connections as you create your palette.

Here, red is the base color. Black accents and low ambient lighting in the crimson field bring drama and excitement to this powder room.

14

Photo: Jenifer Jordan

The swirling patterns in this bath demonstrate a simple complementary color scheme of red-accented green. Note that the red is close to primary while the green has been shaded with black. Though the palette is basic, its effect is sophisticated. Paired with the dark wood of antique furniture and a pewter-finish sink, it evokes a more formal past.

RED

The crown of the color wheel is red. It is the most stimulating and vital color. Traditionally, red is associated with war and courage, love and vengeance. In many cultures, red reads as "stop" or "danger." The ruby, it is said, contains an inextinguishable flame.

Research shows that a person (even a color-blind person) looking at a red wall will show an increase in blood pressure. Red in their surroundings can also stimulate people to be more creative, or to move faster. Advertisers have learned that it can be used in small doses as an exclamation or to pique interest.

Red is considered the warmest color. We read it as very dense; therefore, red objects appear bigger and heavier. Large doses of red on the ceiling or walls may be overpowering, but on the floor or as an accent color it can be quite effective.

The tint of red is pink. While red creates excitement, pink is the most calming of colors. When red is mixed with black, the resulting shade is maroon. As with red, it does not work well in large amounts—it can be morose. As an accent, maroon is very powerful and strong.

BLUE

Blue is second only to red in popularity. It is associated with conservative people and reliability. The painter da Vinci linked blue with the element "air." Many people also relate blue to water and the sea. The sapphire has long been associated with royalty and divine favor.

Blue evokes tranquility, contentment, and meditation. On the other hand, we associate blue with melancholy and sadness. Large areas of blue in a small bathroom may leave you "feeling blue," so select a warm blue or use a warm accent color.

On the walls blue can be restful and tranquil but it can also be cold. Darker shades will make walls seem to recede, but pastel tints of blue make ceilings celestial.

Royal blue accents add sparkle and bring this achromatic bath to life. The many textures add visual interest.

Photo: Laurie Black

Large areas of highly satu-

rated blue get a lift from

splashes of warm color and

vibrating geometric shapes.

There's no chance of creating

a "blue mood" here.

Photo: Tim Street-Porter

GREEN

Green is the result of blue and yellow combined. Of the secondary colors, it is the most harmonious with other colors. Green is a tranquil color; it conjures nature and pastoral scenes. In many cultures green means "Go," and is associated with money.

Green is also connected with the healing arts. Used in the bath, it evokes strong feelings of calm and wellness. Mint green, used alone, can become boring. Add a little yellow to make apple green and you will have the energy needed for a busy morning. Used in large amounts, however, green can create a reflection that is unflattering to the skin.

Although this is essentially a cool green space, accents of red and yellow add excitement to a potentially boring repetition of shapes.

Photo: E. Andrew McKinney

Translucent green stain on the wooden cabinets gives this bath a serene, natural feeling. Amethyst glass introduces another secondary color and texture to the scheme, adding sparkle without upsetting the mood.

A pale tint of yellow opens up this small space with light. The shade is just warm enough to make the room feel cozy.

Photo: Eubanks/Bohnn

YELLOW

Yellow is the third primary color. Cheerful and radiant, sunny yellow is full of bright hope and expectancy. In science, it is associated with intellect and quick thinking. It is the color of spiritual enlightenment in many religions; the Buddha wore yellow. Yellow is the color of gold, suggesting riches and extravagance. This bright and expansive color is the the most light-giving of all hues. Viewing it can increase the metabolic rate. Although it can be used to inspire energy it can also cause hyperactivity.

Light tints of yellow enhance the light in a room. But yellow can also be tricky; if you shade it with too much black, it turns green. If you add too much red, the heat of yellow-orange shades can cause nervousness.

Photo: David Livingston

Glossy purple walls juxtaposed with textured white wainscoting create an exciting backdrop for this collection of ethnic art.

PURPLE

Red and blue mixed together create purple or violet or mauve. "Royal" purple is perceived as regal and dignified. It was the imperial color of Rome and for many centuries was only used by kings and priests. In our own century purple used in interior design was considered gauche. However, during the 1980s fashion turned to bright, multi colors, and brought about a revival in its popularity.

Purple is the color of the dreamer and the artist. Amethyst, the color of wine, once was the chosen color of the god Bacchus and was thought to cure drunkenness.

In its pure form, purple only functions well in interiors as an accent. Tinted to lavender or pale violet it adds charm to a space. Darker shades, however, may affect the eye and be disorienting.

Photo: S. Brooke

ORANGE

Orange is a very modern color. In fact, many cultures view orange and yellow as the same color. It is the color of fire and a definite symbol of energy.

Use orange carefully in bath design; it can easily become loud, or gaudy. On the walls, orange is easier to live with than red, and its reflection is flattering to the skin. If you tint orange with lots of white, the resulting hue matches the inside of a conch shell ... one of the colors in the palette of paradise.

Here a peach tint of orange creates a room filled with flattering light. Tangerine and brass accents bring excitement to the space.

GRAY

True gray is created by mixing black and white. Gray makes a good context or background for other colors, or for art work. Gray is achromatic, meaning "without color." Although it can be very powerful, it can also be dreary and negative. Today many neutral shades are called gray, so be very sure that you are working with a true gray. Since gray has no life of its own, it is essential to use at least a small spot of another color to make the palette work.

The speckled gray effect produces a high-tech look that works well with the strong graphics. The addition of bright yellow makes it zing.

WHITE

White is the presence of all color. You can do almost anything with white. In its pure form, white reflects light and can visually enlarge an area. It can be used to calm intense color and to create a visual resting point. White reads as clean; it enhances any color. However, too much white in a bath can make it sterile looking.

White opens the visual space in this small bath to its maximum. The bright colors of the sink and tile floor are showcased by solid white, and make this rather unremarkable room fun and exciting.

Pristine white tile and glass brick maximize the light in this contemporary bathroom and showcase the intensely colored geometric shapes.

BLACK

High drama, theater, and sophistication are associated with black. Black is the absence of all color. It is the best background to showcase any other color. Use it to make bold accents, but remember that it will absorb light in the room and will show every speck of dust.

These rich, glossy black tiles make a bold statement. Red lines and white lines set up visual vibrations. This bath style would suit a very contemporary person with an aggressive personality.

Photo: R. Greg Hursley

This architecturally rich bathroom combines old and new in a unique way. The black lines darting in many directions are very powerful.

Photo: Mick Hales

Photo: Peter Vitale

This neutral palette is punctuated with black. A wonderful rhythm is set up by the subtle variation of the warm neutrals and the repetition of texture in the baskets and floor.

NEUTRAL TONES

Neutrals include hues from pale beige to taupe to dark brown. They are created by mixing colors and tints and shades. Many people confuse these neutrals with gray. Neutrals have the life that colors give them, gray does not. With neutrals you can create an atmosphere of nature, or showcase bright colors. They can be easy to live with and lived with for a long time. Neutrals swing from warm to cool with more subtlety than pure colors, so they can be deceiving. Match them in the light they will be used in.

Photo: Tim Street-Porter

TEXTURES

Texture can be used as a color in the vocabulary of the mood or statement you are creating. Glossy and slick textures reflect light and have a clean, new look. Polished marble surfaces, mirrors, tiles, windows, and hardware are all excellent choices to reflect and excite. A glossy finish makes rich, dark colors look like jewels and makes light colors sparkle.

Fuzzy and matte textures bring warmth to baths, and make them inviting. Wood, fabrics, towels, rugs, textured walls, and wall coverings are all ways to complement the bath's hard surfaces. However, be aware that these textures also affect the sound and quality of light in the room.

This bath is a masterpiece of the use of textures. Here, black, white and natural tones combine to make a strong, clean graphic statement. The added warmth of wood has primitive appeal.

This high-tech bathroom must be a surfer's dream. The first texture to grab the eye is that of the smooth, corrugated aqua material. Black and white tiles create an opposing pattern that is surely unexpected.

THE GREAT OUTDOORS
Colors from Nature

Photo: Sanitari Pozzi Spa

Lemon and lime combined are as relaxing as a tropical fruit drink. The pastel *mosaic created by the soaps and repeated in the tub border tickle your fancy.*

Whether in the city or the country, this palette is for those inspired by sunset views. These baths reflect the passing seasons, from new buds to falling leaves. Colors as pure as the petals of flowers and natural hues and textures make up this palette.

● **THE GREAT OUTDOORS PALETTE**

This palette is as changeable as the environment; the colors within it can create effects that are fragile and fresh or designs with an earthy strength. The palette is evenly divided between the springlike energy of leaf green and ocean blue, and the autumnal tones of goldenrod and brick red.

 Leaf Green

 Ocean Blue

 Slate Gray

 Goldenrod

 Brick Red

In this bath, materials bring the colors and textures of the painted desert into the room. Although the colors are pale, the natural tile requires no further ornament.

Photo: Tim Street-Porter

Photo: Dennis Jenkins

Mosaic Blue

Terra-Cotta

The shine of clear blue tile against matte terra-cotta paving stones works to create a rich harmony of color and texture.

Sand

Butterscotch

Photo: Giarusso & Associates

Natural colors and accessories blend a serene and luxurious bath with its natural surroundings. The monochrome scheme works because of the varieties of texture.

 Cherry

 Marigold

Honey Dew

The leaf green light and marigold accents in this city bath evoke an emerald forest.

 Tangerine

Midnight Blue

Natural greenery puts an earthy spin on the contemporary colors of this bath.

Photo: Timothy Hursley

Photo: Hickey-Robertson

Melon Gold

Foliage Green

Silk, marble, and plush carpet blend the elegance of an off-white palette with the greenery of nature.

Brick Red

Melon Gold

This bath gives a sophisticated city dwelling a window on nature; a back-drop of pale cream draws attention to the greenery and jewel colors of the environment. The brick red bank of tile links the bathing area to the colors in the adjacent room.

Photo: Jenifer Jordan

Slate Gray

Marigold

*Deep colors, black
tile, and heavy
materials create a
wonderful, cavelike
atmosphere. Plenty
of natural light and
yellow tones in the
stone keep the dark
walls from closing
in visually.*

Photo: Hickey-Robertson

Terra-Cotta

Slate Gray

The elements of this bath appear monochromatic. However, nature has sprinkled the marble tile with terra-cotta and gray, which creates subtle energy.

Primary Blue

Buttermilk

Sunflower Yellow

Photo: Hickey-Robertson

Mauve

Driftwood Gray

Lots of natural light, monochromatic white-on-white tile, and driftwood gray woodwork open the walls of this bath, making an airy backdrop for a collection of antique bird cages.

Photo: Geoffrey Gross   Designer: T. Keller Donavon

*Primary yellow and
blue in the rug are the
foundation for the color
scheme here. By using tints
of these colors in large areas,
the palette blends well with
the natural surroundings.*

Photo: Timothy Hursley

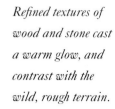

Marble Gray

Mahogany

Refined textures of wood and stone cast a warm glow, and contrast with the wild, rough terrain.

Vine Green

Sand Stone

Neutral color paired with bold texture makes a small area feel larger. The shiny mirror surface complements the rough stone and wood.

Photo: Lou Ann Bauer, ASID

Lagoon Blue

Beach

In this room,
the colors reflect
the hues of a
warm sand beach
lapped with
turquoise waters.

Photo: Paul Warchol

THE HOME FIRES
Colors That Glow

Saturated yellow gives the walls of this bath a sunny intensity. Using this much pigment in a small room takes imagination and courage, but the results can be truly outstanding.

Photo: Sanitari Pozzi Spa

This palette creates places of refuge; its deep, saturated hues are ideal for those who want their home to be their haven. The colors in this group warm and visually enhance the space. Soft textures and attention to ambient lighting bring out the best in these warm colors.

Photo: Smallbone

● THE HOME FIRES PALETTE

Warm shades such as flame red, pumpkin, and harvest yellow radiate flattering light in the small space of the bath. Heather purple and classic blue cool the heat of the other colors in this palette but are still vivid enough to stand on their own.

 Flame Red

 Pumpkin

 Harvest Yellow

 Heather Purple

 Classic Blue

A brilliant glaze lights the walls of this bath. Glazes allow the background wall color to show through, making even saturated colors look soft.

Photo: Balthazar Korab

Cherry

Taupe

Though it appears to be gray, the color in this bath is actually a light tint of taupe —blue, red, and yellow mixed together in nearly equal amounts. The primary colors create a neutral shade that still has energy and warmth. The accent color here is red—pure, shaded, and tinted.

Flame Red

Pumpkin

Classic Blue

Photo: Hickey-Robertson

The flame-stitched colors

of this bath's wallpaper

suggest autumn leaves.

Glinting brass accents add

fire to the warm palette.

Photo: Timothy Hursley

Mahogany

Mustard Yellow

The warmth of natural wood makes an inviting island in this glass and metal loft. Notice how the ambient incandescent light imitates the glow of firelight.

Mahogany

Brass

Red Ember

Here, the rich, ruddy tones of mahogany paneling act like saturated red, absorbing light and visually enclosing this space. Sparkling brass brings highlights to the bath.

Watermelon

Rose

Moss Green

Hunter green walls are a perfect back-ground for a warm floral palette. Red, even when it is lightened to this pale tint of rose, casts a soft glow.

Cherry

Leaf Green

Black is a powerful showcase for colors. Here it emphasizes the visual energy of red, purple, and yellow-green in the patterned wallpaper.

Photo: Kohler

Powder Blue

Buttermilk

Sumptuous creamy surfaces soften the dark impact of walnut fixtures. Touches of blue match the evening sky.

Photo: Balthazar Korab

Delft Blue

Dusty Rose

You can use blue and white abundantly and still avoid creating a cold atmosphere, if you warm the palette with rose accents.

Photo: Hedrich-Blessing

Photo: Paul Warchol

Photo: Timothy Hursley

Flame Red

Yellow Straw

Citrus

Warm Wood

Classic Blue

The dull shine of silvered walls brightens this bath alcove. A wash of straw yellow enlivens the ceiling and fills the room with sunny light.

Red-Orange

Mahogany

One fascinating thing about this bathroom is that the wood finish and the marble are so close to the same hue. The impact of a red-orange and white palette is heightened by using it to cover all surfaces.

Photo: Timothy Hursley

To pull together a wide range of neutrals in a room, use color as a focal point. In this bath, colorful prints perform the task.

FARAWAY PLACES
Colors of the World

Photo: MB Associates

Mirrors and a trompe l'oeil balcony enlarge this area enough to visu- ally accommodate the dark floor and a large antique commode.

O ceans of blue, the bone white of a Greek village bleaching in the sun, reds and orange from a Moroccan bazaar—these are the colors of the world. From Katmandu to Belize, people are fascinated by other cultures. The colors in this group can be used to weave an exotic tapestry. Accessories will strengthen designs created with this palette; think of handmade tiles, ethnic art, and finishes not usually found in the bath.

● FARAWAY PLACES
PALETTE

Since they absorb light, the deep red and black of this palette can be used to create an atmosphere of drama and mystery. Caribbean blue, and its complement, mandarin orange, are versatile; rich, jewel tones at full saturation, they can also be paled to tints that reflect light and visually enlarge the space.

 Ebony

Bone White

 Caribbean Blue

 Mandarin Orange

 Lacquer Red

Photo: Jenifer Jordan

Black and white with red is usually a dramatic combination. This design takes its cues from the Far East, using white-washed wood to give the colors a natural, tranquil flow.

Mahogany

Brass

Ivory

The ornate surfaces and rich natural hues of this bath suggest an African Palace. Range of color—from darkest dark to lightest light—is one of the reasons this design is so successful.

Photo: Peter Vitale

Chinese Red

Ebony

In this exotic bath, black and Chinese red convey drama and mystery. Since these colors do not reflect light, add shiny surfaces or gold accents to do so.

Photo: Jenifer Jordan

Hibiscus Red

Pumpkin

Primary and secondary colors are strung together like carnival beads on these dancing tiles. Notice how little the predominance of minty green and golden pine does to cool the accent colors.

Ebony

Aquamarine

Redwood

Photo: R. Greg Hursley

Pale, natural hues keep this space from being overpow-ered by the dark trim. The intense primitive design uses blues and reds muddied almost to the value of earth tones.

Photo: Tim Street-Porter

Slate Gray

Cranberry

Storm Blue

The consistent use of blue and green accents in a slate and red palette makes this color scheme unique. Snakeskin- patterned wallpaper and a hanging bird cage add a mystical quality to the room.

Wheat

Ebony

Lapis Blue

*Ebony details give
a neutral bath
powerful impact.
High gloss paint is
used to beautiful
effect and creates
the impression
of inlaid wood.*

Photo: Giarusso and Associates

61

Moroccan Red

Coast Blue

*Blocks of color
define a narrow
space. The exalted
palette of gold leaf,
cobalt, and lacquer
red is amusing in
this tiny space.*

Photo: Dan Forer Photography

Cream

Teal

This shade of blue looks exotic no matter where it is used. Strategically placed white and pale yellow enhance the deep color, and keep it true to the shade in the stained glass window.

Photo: James A. W. Ear Photography

Cream

Raspberry Sherbet

Light colors can still have rich tones, as demonstrated by the range of cream shades in this bath.

Agate

Pineapple Mist

In this tranquil bath design, prints add the needed color and their subject carries out the design theme. The bone-marbled tile intensifies the neutral colors in the room.

Photo: Timothy Hursley

Aqua

Cherry

These vintage tiles carry a primitive color scheme of aqua, red, and black. Contrary to the modern convention of carefully matched hues, here each surface carries its own interpretation of the palette. The doors, floor tiles, and ceiling are all different variations of the same theme.

Mahogany

Ebony

Sleek baths like this one can look Spartan. Here, gold burnishes the walls, and henna red woodwork glows like African coals.

Photo: Tim Street-Porter

THE UNEXPECTED
Colors That Surprise

Photo: Paul Warchol

A plain room calls for "Wow!" color. The strong shade of green becomes a focus in this spare bath.

Straight from left field, these bold colors are anything but predictable. This bright palette makes an old room look new, and a new one modern. Creative and fun, the Unexpected palette is for real individuals. Here, anything goes—incongruous uses of materials and colors are the rule, not the exception.

● THE UNEXPECTED PALETTE

This palette gets power from its energetic secondary colors. Rainbow-hued for the most part, these colors work their magic by giving a room atmosphere. Materials contribute to the element of surprise; the texture of cement, or tones of copper, bring another unusual dimension to unexpected color.

 Chartreuse

 Peacock Teal

 Flag Blue

 Holly Berry Red

 Dark Chocolate

Touches of bright pink give masculine, steel gray hues a more feminine outlook.

Photo: The Gura Agency

69

Sunshine Yellow

Hot Red

Milk Chocolate

Taking a palette from a work of art is a great place to start. This room uses colors in almost the same proportions as the print. The theatrical dressing area carries out the theme.

Brass

Copper

Wild Iris

Mocha

Most of the colors in this palette are from the array of metals —copper, brass, gold, and cobalt. The wall colors echo the metal hues.

Photo: Studio Verde/Acquario Due Sas

Photo: Paul Warchol

This achromatic room changes levels, not colors, to create surprise. The granite is a collection of all of the other tones in the bathroom.

Parchment

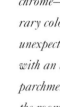

Ebony

Black and white and chrome—a contemporary color scheme is unexpectedly combined with an antique parchment hue, giving the room an old-world feeling.

ottle Green

ly Berry Red

Complementary red and green, combined with a large expanse of white, is very refreshing. To make this combination work, use the saturated colors sparingly.

Photo: Mick Hales

Hot Red

Canary

Medium Brown

*The rough textures
and natural colors
of the building ma-
terials make these
shiny bright reds
and yellows all
the more surreal
in this artist's loft.*

Photo: Balthazar Korab

Photo: Balthazar Korab

Spring Yellow-Green

Terra-Cotta

Lavender Pink

Aqua

*The slightly irregular
values in each hand-
made tile in this
vintage bath create
a wonderful patina.
The original pink
and aqua palette
was shocking in its
era and is widely
imitated today.*

Photo: Timothy Hursley

The sumptuous colors of the glass are played to by the neutrals in this quirky bath design. Glittering areas throughout the room keep the eye in constant motion.

Photo: Smallbone

Claret

Willow Green

Julep Green

Shades of green frame the classic profiles of twin sculptures. Brilliant red emphasizes an Aubusson rug, highlighting the surprise of finding it in the bath.

Sometimes breaking a rule can create powerful design. In this white-on-white room, the focus becomes the old fixtures and architectural elements because there is no accent color.

Photo: Paul Warchol

 Stratosphere Blue

 Chrome

 Aquamarine Blue

"Color and light,
color and light …"
The trick to creating
this fantasy bath is
done with mirrors.

Photo: Van Inwegan Photography

Photo: Paul Warchol

Photo: James Wilson Photography

Eraser Pink

Putty

Photo: Timothy Hursley

Wedgewood Blue

Limestone

Sea Green

Plain blue paired with cream makes a space-age design user friendly.

Wood

Warm Taupe

Blue Wash

Wood, brick, tile, chrome, and Lucite … each of these elements brings a different color to this Spartan bath and reflects the light differently— creating a dream- like effect.

The use of the unexpected is a very effective design trick. Soft pink in this rough-finished area is a pleasant surprise.

GRAPHIC
Colors That Define

Photo Tim Street-Porter

Handmade tiles echo the texture of the bamboo. Their cream color, *the yellow of the bamboo, and the yellow translucent roof make up a* *monochrome palette, with black tiles standing in sharp graphic contrast.*

Graphic color schemes give architecture a boost. This palette uses contrast to give odd spaces visual organiza-tion and lends interest to ordinary spaces. Putting messages on the walls started with the cave man. Today, graphic colors are the messages of design; they define edges and draw the viewer's eye.

● GRAPHIC PALETTE

This palette uses a simple idea —juxtaposing a light color with a darker one—to make a bold statement. Some Graphic designs also rely on repetition for their success, picking up a single color in a scheme and repeating it to give unity to the space.

 Metal

 Periwinkle Blue

 Bubble Gum

 Daffodil Yellow

 Turf Green

These tinted colors have high energy without being loud. The patterned band segues from one color to the other, holding the room together visually.

Photo: Ideal Standard Spa

Photo: Timothy Hursley

Lavender

Olive Green

This bath's mosaic combines geometric and organic shapes with the flowing architecture.

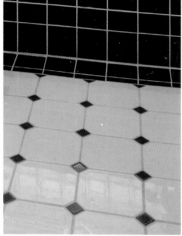

Navy Blue

Terra Cotta

Small terra-cotta tiles introduce the surprise of ruddy tones and a hint of nature to this otherwise high-tech palette.

Photo: R. Greg Hursley

Photo: Paul Warchol

Granite

Stone

Photo: Parker and Rogers

Pale Celery

Oak

Stainless Steel

The juxtaposition of pale celery and natural oak with stainless steel brings tension to an otherwise bland space. Light reflecting from shiny surfaces keeps the room cheerful and bright.

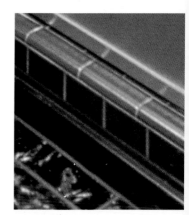

Black and mahogany make a strong statement, but the clever, subtle use of white in all of the black surfaces reflects enough light to give the whole area energy.

Photo: Tim Street-Porter

Robin's Egg

Asparagus

Hot Red

Tile is an ancient art medium. This freestyle mosaic manipulates colors with the intricacy of an oil painting.

Black Metal

Cherry

Sulfur

*Extending a red
and yellow super-
graphic over the
glass is a creative
surprise. The colors
are a deliberate
contrast to the nat-
ural background.*

Photo: Hickey-Robertson

Sky Blue

Oak

Stainless Steel

The panel of sky blue adjacent to the real sky makes a clever point of interest. The sterility of white and stainless steel are softened in color and texture by the wood and onyx.

Photo: Paul Warchol

Red Crayon

Butterscotch

Soft Gray

A simple and beautiful room takes its energy from the repeated band around the counter and in the rug.

Cool Taupe

Rouge

Photo: Hickey-Robertson

Colors for Living • **BATHS** • Graphic

Cobalt Blue

Bleached Wood

Turf Green

Cobalt blue perimeter lines and an oversized mirror visually enlarge this area. Cool blue and white are warmed by the natural woods.

Photo: Paul Warchol

90

Color takes a back seat here to the art deco design. There is so much going on in the design that color would just add confusion. Note, however, that the warm pink veining brings the marble countertop to life.

Harvest Yellow

Easter Pink

Air Force Blue

Our field of color perception has been increased by neon lights, video, and laser rays. This room is an expression of space-age art.

Photo: Timothy Hursley

Photo: Timothy Hursley

Foam Green

Hunter Green

The focal point of this bath is a fabulous glass etching. As with the city of its inspiration, the colors change all day with the light.

Air Force Blue

Grape

Verdigris

Using these massive areas of color in a utilitarian space is Bauhaus-inspired. These dreamy, water colors around a sunken tub promote relaxation.

Photo: Hickey-Robertson

TRANQUILITY
Colors That Calm

This clean-lined vertical architecture is accentuated by red horizontal lines on the cream field.

Photo: Ceramica Sant' Agostino Spa

U se the neutrals and pale shades of blue in this palette to make a bath into a safe harbor. Inspired by the pale spectrum of morning light, these colors bring soft light into a room, transforming it into a place of renewal.

Cloud Gray

Sand

Conch Pink

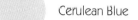
Cerulean Blue

Deep Sea Blue

Photo: Hedrich-Blessing

The concept of this design is contradiction. Santa Fe— style architecture is mixed with contemporary. The palette is a mixture of the desert neutrals and the sunset pastels.

Ebony

Vanilla

*This achromatic
room is warmed by
the ambient lighting.
The repetition of
pattern adds energy.*

Photo: R. Greg Hursley

Warm Taupe

Silver Cloud

Raspberry

Photo: Kohler

A mixture of warm taupes and exotic textures wrap the viewer in a feeling of tranquility. The raspberry is very effective because it is used so sparingly.

Photo: Jenifer Jordan

Sapphire Blue

Robin's Egg

This is a heavenly room. Painting the sky on the ceiling was a very creative way to enhance the mood begun by the lovely blue and white tiles.

affodil Yellow

Slate Gray

Metal

Rich materials and textures are the overriding theme of this bathroom. The small accent of clear yellow dictates the personality of the room. Imagine how different it would look if the flowers and soap were red or bright purple.

Photo: Eubanks/Bohnn

Photo: R. Greg Hursley

Seafoam

Bone

Stark contemporary style is very cleverly handled here. The materials of this Spartan bathroom are all hard and cool. Yet the palette of warm blue and taupe and the soft light coming through the glass make it inviting.

Sand

Conch Pink

Seashells are most appropriately displayed against the color of the beach. This monochromatic scheme works without an accent color because the light playing off the mirrors adds visual energy.

Photo: Hickey-Robertson

Air Force Blue

Natural Wood

Warm Taupe

Cool Taupe

*In this airy bath-
room the neutral
tile ranges in hue
from warm to cool.
The warm is com-
plememented by
the pine beams
and the cool by
the blue table.*

Photo: Timothy Hursley

Cascade Blue

Khaki

Elaborate textures work together to build this soft haven. Warm blue as the color accent enhances the serene mood.

Photo: Tim Street-Porter

Ebony

Cobalt Blue

Natural Wood

Images of white linen and lawn parties are conjured up by this bathroom. The basic room of black and white is architecturally interesting but it could be harsh. By adding warm, neutral tones and textures the room is softened and taken back in time. The cobalt blue gives that one sparkle of color that adds life.

Cool Taupe

Boysenberry

Cool taupe marble with warm-hued veining is repeated in the mauve and blue fabric. This palette is very soothing.

Photo: Kohler

Slate Gray

Aquamarine

Beach

Photo: James A. Wilson Photography

Japanese design philosophy was the guide for this tranquil space. The dark floor represents earth, the natural wood, life, and the palest of blue is heaven.

Photo: Timothy Hursley

Copper

Sandstone

In this executive washroom a feeling of nature is brought to the big city. Soft neutral colors and textures offer a respite from cold steel and cement.

Silver

Ebony

Dark Wood

Black and silver make a very powerful and dramatic statement. The touch of silky, dark wood makes the space inviting.

Photo: Paul Warchol

Our special thanks to those photographers, architects, and designers who graciously contributed their work to make this book a reality.

PHOTOGRAPHERS

Arch/ Balthazar Korab Ltd.

Lou Anne Bauer, ASID

Laurie Black

Hedrich Blessing

Stephen Brooke

Ceramica Saint'Agostino Spa

Martin Fine Photography

Dan Forer Photography

Geoffrey Gross

The Gura Agency

Mick Hales

Hastings Tile & Il Bagno Collection

Paul Hester

R. Greg Hursley

Timothy Hursley

Dennis Jenkins Associates

Jenifer Jordan

Elliott Kaufman

Kohler

David Livingston

David Lund

MB Associates

E. Andrew McKinney

Joseph Minton

Lanny Provo

Hickey-Robertson Photography

Parker & Rodgers

Sanitari Pozzi Spa

SmallBone Cabinetry

Tim Street-Porter

Peter Vitale

Paul Warchol

Nancy Robinson Watson

Van In Wegen Photography

James Wilson

WilsonArt

ARCHITECTS/ DESIGNERS

Bauer Interior Design

Chele Benjamin, Designer

Eric Bernard

Kutnicki/Bernstein Architects

Nolan Blass

Bommarito Design Group

Booziotis Architect

William Bruder Architect

Bryan Design Associates, Mary Ann Bryan, ASID & Joan Portman, ASID & Diana Walker, ASID & Kay White, ASID & Jan Thompson, ASID & Sarah Brooks Eilers, ASID

Anita Carpenter, Interior Designer

Dick Clark, AIA Architect

Richard Davis, Architect

Norman Dehaan Designer

T. Keller Donovan, Designer NYC

Tony Duquette

Eubanks/Bohnn

Gay Fly

Dianne Garrett, Interior Designer

Giarusso & Associates

Gilbreath Designer

Richard Gluckman Architects

Donna Guerra Designs

Hariri & Hariri

Steven Harris

Margaret Helfand Architect

Frank Israel Architect

Dennis Jenkins Associates

Kevin Kosiek, Creators of Wonder

Lake/Flato Architects, San Antonio, TX/ Don Crowell, Contractor

Mark Mack

MB Associates Interior Design/Bianca O. Figuerda & Associates

Bobby McAlpine

Francois de Menil Architect

Moore/Anderson Architects

Carolyn Mosher

MRY Architects

Mickey Muehnig

Brian Murphy

Rosa Palma

David Rockwell & Jay Haverson Architects (Formerly Haverson Rockwell)

Janet Schirn Design Group

Barbara Schlattman, ASID, Barbara Schlattman Interiors, Inc., Houston, TX

Harriet Schneider, HSS Design

Peter Shire

Gwathmey Siegel & Associates

Stamberg Aferiat Architecture

Alexi Steele Fine Art Studio/Muralist

Robert A.M. Stern, Architect

Stiles and Clements, Architects

Zihua Tanejo

Charles Tapley, FAIA

Michael Taylor

Three Architecture, Inc.

Larry Totah

Robin Weiss, Interior Designer

Tricia Wilson & Associates

Kevin Young, Designer

COLOR
SWATCHES

Chapter 1 — Main Palette THE GREAT OUTDOORS *Colors From Nature*	TINTS	SHADES
Leaf Green	Tinted Leaf Green	Shaded Leaf Green
Ocean Blue	Tinted Ocean Blue	Shaded Ocean Blue
Slate Gray	Tinted Slate Gray	Shaded Slate Gray
Goldenrod	Tinted Goldenrod	Shaded Goldenrod
Brick Red	Tinted Brick Red	Shaded Brick Red

THE HOME FIRES
Colors That Glow

TINTS

SHADES

Flame Red	Tinted Flame Red	Shaded Flame Red
Pumpkin	Tinted Pumpkin	Shaded Pumpkin
Harvest Yellow	Tinted Harvest Yellow	Shaded Harvest Yellow
Heather Purple	Tinted Heather Purple	Shaded Heather Purple
Classic Blue	Tinted Classic Blue	Shaded Classic Blue

Chapter 3 — Main Palette	TINTS	SHADES
FARAWAY PLACES *Colors of the World*		
Ebony	Tinted Ebony	
Bone White	Tinted Bone White	Shaded Bone White
Caribbean Blue	Tinted Caribbean Blue	Shaded Caribbean Blue
Mandarin Orange	Tinted Mandarin Orange	Shaded Mandarin Orange
Lacquer Red	Tinted Lacquer Red	Shaded Lacquer Red

THE UNEXPECTED		TINTS		SHADES	
Chapter 4 — Main Palette					

THE UNEXPECTED
Colors That Surprise

	Color		Tinted		Shaded
	Chartreuse		Tinted Chartreuse		Shaded Chartreuse
	Peacock Teal		Tinted Peacock Teal		Shaded Peacock Teal
	Flag Blue		Tinted Flag Blue		Shaded Flag Blue
	Holly Berry Red		Tinted Holly Berry Red		Shaded Holly Berry Red
	Dark Chocolate		Tinted Dark Chocolate		Shaded Dark Chocolate

GRAPHIC	TINTS	SHADES

Chapter 5 — Main Palette
GRAPHIC
Colors That Define

TINTS

SHADES

Metal	Tinted Metal	Shaded Metal
Periwinkle Blue	Tinted Periwinkle Blue	Shaded Periwinkle Blue
Bubblegum	Tinted Bubblegum	Shaded Bubblegum
Daffodil Yellow	Tinted Daffodil Yellow	Shaded Daffodil Yellow
Turf Green	Tinted Turf Green	Shaded Turf Green

Chapter 6 — Main Palette TRANQUILITY *Colors That Calm*		TINTS		SHADES	
	Cloud Gray		Tinted Cloud Gray		Shaded Cloud Gray
	Sand		Tinted Sand		Shaded Sand
	Conch Pink		Tinted Conch Pink		Shaded Conch Pink
	Cerulean Blue		Tinted Cerulean Blue		Shaded Cerulean Blue
	Deep Sea Blue		Tinted Deep Sea Blue		Shaded Deep Sea Blue

Mosaic Blue Page 32	Honey Dew Page 35	Driftwood Gray Page 40
Terra-Cotta Page 32, 39	Tangerine Page 35	Primary Blue Page 40
Sand Page 32	Midnight Blue Page 35	Buttermilk Page 40
Butterscotch Page 32	Melon Gold Page 36, 37	Sunflower Yellow Page 40
Cherry Page 35	Foliage Green Page 36	Vine Green Page 42
Marigold Page 35, 38	Mauve Page 40	Sand Stone Page 42

Marble Gray Page 42	Mahogany Page 48	Moss Green Page 49
Mahogany Page 42	Brass Page 48	Leaf Green Page 50
Lagoon Blue Page 43	Red Ember Page 48	Powder Blue Page 50
Beach Page 43	Mustard Yellow Page 48	Buttermilk Page 50
Cherry Page 46, 50	Watermelon Page 49	Delft Blue Page 51
Taupe Page 46	Rose Page 49	Dusty Rose Page 51

	Red-Orange Page 52		Ivory Page 56		Slate Gray Page 60
	Yellow Straw Page 52		Chinese Red Page 57		Cranberry Page 60
	Warm Wood Page 52		Hibiscus Red Page 58		Storm Blue Page 60
	Citrus Page 52		Pumpkin Page 58		Wheat Page 61
	Mahogany Page 56, 67		Aquamarine Page 58		Lapis Blue Page 61
	Brass Page 56		Redwood Page 58		Moroccan Red Page 62

	Coast Blue Page 62		Aqua Page 66		Copper Page 71
	Cream Page 63, 64		Cherry Page 66		Wild Iris Page 71
	Teal Page 63		Sunshine Yellow Page 70		Mocha Page 71
	Agate Page 64		Hot Red Page 70		Bottle Green Page 72
	Pineapple Mist Page 64		Milk Chocolate Page 70		Parchment Page 73
	Raspberry Sherbet Page 64		Brass Page 71		Ebony Page 73

Hot Red Page 74	Terra-Cotta Page 74	Aquamarine Blue Page 77
Canary Page 74	Claret Page 76	Wedgewood Blue Page 78
Medium Brown Page 74	Willow Green Page 76	Limestone Page 78
Lavender Pink Page 74	Julep Green Page 76	Sea Green Page 78
Aqua Page 74	Stratosphere Blue Page 77	Eraser Pink Page 78
Spring Yellow-Green Page 74	Chrome Page 77	Putty Page 78

	Wood Page 78	Terra-Cotta Page 83	Robin's Egg Page 86
	Warm Taupe Page 78	Pale Celery Page 84	Asparagus Page 86
	Blue Wash Page 78	Oak Page 84, 88	Hot Red Page 86
	Lavender Page 82	Stainless Steel Page 84, 88	Black Metal Page 87
	Olive Green Page 82	Granite Page 84	Cherry Page 87
	Navy Blue Page 83	Stone Page 84	Sulfur Page 87

	Sky Blue Page 88		Cool Taupe Page 90		Verdigris Page 93
	Red Crayon Page 89		Rouge Page 90		Foam Green Page 93
	Butterscotch Page 89		Harvest Yellow Page 92		Hunter Green Page 93
	Soft Gray Page 89		Easter Pink Page 92		Ebony Page 96
	Cobalt Blue Page 90		Air Force Blue Page 92, 93		Vanilla Page 96
	Bleached Wood Page 90		Grape Page 93		Warm Taupe Page 96

	Silver Cloud Page 96		Robin's Egg Page 99		Cascade Blue Page 103
	Raspberry Page 96		Seafoam Page 100		Khaki Page 103
	Daffodil Yellow Page 99		Bone Page 100		Boysenberry Page 104
	Slate Gray Page 99, 104		Air Force Blue Page 102		Cobalt Blue Page 104
	Metal Page 99		Natural Wood Page 102, 104		Aquamarine Page 104
	Sapphire Blue Page 99		Cool Taupe Page 102, 104		Beach Page 104

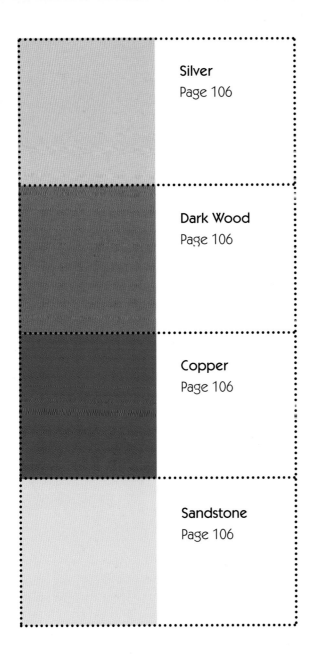

Silver
Page 106

Dark Wood
Page 106

Copper
Page 106

Sandstone
Page 106

COLOR GLOSSARY

Analogous Color Scheme — A scheme that uses three colors (or their tints and shades) that are next to each other on the color wheel.

Chroma — Chroma is the degree of brilliance of a color.

Complementary Color Scheme — A color scheme that uses colors from opposite sides of the color wheel.

Hue — Hue is the formal term for color.

Monochromatic Color Scheme — A color scheme that uses only variations of one color, or a scheme that uses only white, black, and gray.

Saturation — Saturation is the intensity or brightness of a color.

Shades — Shades (or dark values) are colors with black added to them.

Split Complementary Scheme — A color scheme made up of any color combined with two colors on either side of its complement on the color wheel.

Temperature — The perceived warmth or coolness of a color.

Tints — Tints (or light tonal values) are colors with white added to them.

Triad Color Scheme — A color scheme that uses three colors (or their tints or shades) that are equidistant on the color wheel.

Value — Value (or tonal value) is the relative lightness or darkness of a color.

BIBLIOGRAPHY

Albers, Josef. *Interaction of Color.* New Haven: Yale University, 1963.

Birren, Faber. *Color in Your World.* New York: Collier Books, 1962.

Birren, Faber. *Color and Human Response.* New York: Van Nostrand Reinhold Company, 1978.

Chijiiwa, Hideaki. *Color Harmony: A Guide to Creative Color Combinations.* Rockport, MA: Rockport Publishers, 1987.

Conran, Terence. *The Bed and Bath Book.* New York: Crown Publishers Inc., 1978.

Gilliatt, Mary. *Bathrooms.* New York: The Viking Press, Inc., 1971.

Kunz, George Frederick. *The Curious Lore of Precious Stones.* New York, Dover Publications, Inc., 1913.

Luscher, Max. *The Luscher Color Test.* New York: Washington Square Press Publication, 1969.

Mazzurco, Philip. *Bath Design.* New York: Whitney Library of Design, 1986.

Mejetta, Mirko and Simonetta Spada. *Interiors in Color: Creating Space, Personality and Atmosphere.* New York: Whitney Library of Design, 1983.

Mella, Dorothee L. *The Language of Color.* New York: Warner Books, 1988.

Niesewand, Nonie. *Conran's Bedrooms and Bathrooms.* Boston: Little, Brown and Company, 1986.

Powell, William F. *Color and How to Use It.* Tustin, CA: Walter Foster Publishing, 1984.

Stoddard, Alexandra. *Alexandra Stoddard's Book of Color.* New York: Doubleday, 1989.

Using Color and Light. Des Moines, IA: Better Homes and Gardens Books, 1985.

DIRECTORY OF BATHROOM SUPPLIERS & MANUFACTURERS

Acquario Due s.a.s.
di Zancanella Federico & C.
via Euganea, 35
35037 Treponti di Teolo (PD)
Italy

Agostinelli snc
di Alberto e Sergio Agostinelli
Via S. Maria del Rosario 8
20032 Cormano (MI)
Italy

Allmilmö Corp.
P.O. Box 629
70 Clinton Road
Fairfield, NJ 07004-2976

Jean-Marie Beyers
rue VanderKindere straat 546
B-1180 Bruxelles
Belgium

Boffi Spa
Via G Oberdan
20030 Lentate Sul Seveso
Milano
Italy

Ceramica Catalano
Strada Privinciale Falerina
Km 7200
01034 Fabrica di Roma(VT)
Italy

Ceramica Sant'Agostino Spa
V. Statale 247
44047 S. Agostino
Ferrara
Italy

Mileweski Mobelwerk
Obere Altack #1
97475-ZEIL AM MAIN
Germany

Duravit AG
Postfach 240
78128 Hornberg
NL

Genio s.n.c.
via Pietro Custodi 10
20136 Milano
Italy

Grohe
900 Lively Boulevard
Wood Dale, Il 60191

Hastings Tile- Il Bagno Collection
30 Commercial Street
Freeport, NY 11520

Ideal Standard SPA
20131 Milano Via Ampere 102
Casella Postale 930
Milano
Italy

Italian Tile Center
The Italian Trade Commission
499 Park Avenue
New York, New York 10022

Italian Tile Center
via Liszt- 21
00144 Rome
ITALY

JADO Bath & Hardware Mfg. Co.
P.O. Box 1329
1690 Calle Quetzal
Camarillo, CA 93011

Jacuzzi Europe spa
SS. Pontebbana Km 97200
33098 Valvasone (PN)
Italy

Kallista
1355 Market Street
San Francisco, CA 94103

Kermi
egeda sa
Industriezone Wolfstee
Toekomstlaan 47
2200 Herentals
Belgium

Kohler Company
Kohler, WI 53044

KWC
Rohl Corporation
1559 Sunland Lane
Costa Mesa, CA 92626

Marbrerie Crombe
sa/nv
Ch. de Haecht 1465
Haachtsesteenweg
1130 Bruxelles, Brussels
Belgium

Moab 80 srl
Via Vaccheria di Gianni 93
00155 Roma
Italy

Neomediam
Z.I. des Ecrevolles - B.P. 2024
10010 Troyes Cedex
France

Porcher
3618 East LaSalle
Pheonix, AZ 85040

Sanijura s.a.
Parc indistriel
6220 Fleurus
France

Nortesco Inc.
57 Galaxy Blvd.
Unit 5 Toronto
Rexdale M9W5P1
Canada

Sanitari Pozzi SPA
viale Giulio Richard,1
Milano
Italy

Smallbone Inc.
886 Town Center Drive
Langhorne, PA 19047

室 • Banyolar • 화장실들 • I Bagni • שרותים

adkamers • ห้องน้ำหลายห้อง • Les salles de b

as De Banho • Bathrooms • 浴室 • Los Baños

浴室 • Banyolar • 화장실들 • I Bagni • שרותים

dezimmer • Badkamers • ห้องน้ำหลายห้อง • I

רותי • שCasas De Banho • Bathrooms • 浴室

es salles de bains • 浴室 • Banyolar • 화장실들

os Baños • Badezimmer • Badkamers • ห้องน้ำ

장실들 • I Bagni • שרותים • Casas De Banho

ห้องน้ำหลายห้อง • Les salles de bains • 浴室 •

throoms • 浴室 • Los Baños • Badezimmer •

anyolar • 화장실들 • I Bagni • שרותים • Casa

dkamers • ห้องน้ำหลายห้อง • Les salles de ba

Bathrooms • 浴室 • Los Baños • Badezimmer

Banyolar • 화장실들 • I Bagni שרותים